budgetbooks

POP/ROCK

ISBN 978-0-634-04072-6

HAL•LEONARD®

Visit Hal Leonard Online at
www.halleonard.com

Contact us:
Hal Leonard
7777 West Bluemound Road
Milwaukee, WI 53213
Email: info@halleonard.com

In Europe, contact:
Hal Leonard Europe Limited
42 Wigmore Street
Marylebone, London, W1U 2RN
Email: info@halleonardeurope.com

In Australia, contact:
Hal Leonard Australia Pty. Ltd.
4 Lentara Court
Cheltenham, Victoria, 3192 Australia
Email: info@halleonard.com.au

CONTENTS

ABC

Words and Music by ALPHONSO MIZELL, FREDERICK PERREN,
DEKE RICHARDS and BERRY GORDY

ADIA

Words and Music by SARAH McLACHLAN
and PIERRE MARCHAND

9

CRIMSON AND CLOVER

Words and Music by TOMMY JAMES
and PETER LUCIA

18

ANGEL

Words and Music by
SARAH McLACHLAN

Original key: D♭ major. This edition has been transposed down one half-step to be more playable.

BABY WHAT A BIG SURPRISE

Words and Music by
PETER CETERA

BACK IN THE HIGH LIFE AGAIN

Words and Music by WILL JENNINGS
and STEVE WINWOOD

BAD, BAD LEROY BROWN

Words and Music by
JIM CROCE

BARBARA ANN

Words and Music by
FRED FASSERT

BARELY BREATHING

Words and Music by
DUNCAN SHEIK

BEN

Words by DON BLACK
Music by WALTER SCHARF

Ben, the two of us need look no more. We both found what we were look-ing for. With a friend to call my own, I'll nev-er be a-

CENTERFOLD

Written by
SETH JUSTMAN

54

DIZZY

Words and Music by TOMMY ROE
and FREDDY WELLER

EVERY HEARTBEAT

Words and Music by AMY GRANT,
WAYNE KIRKPATRICK and CHARLIE PEACOCK

Hear me speak what's on my mind.
Clas- sic case of boy meets girl.

Let me give this
Mov- ing in the

tes- ti- mon- y.
same di- rec- tion.

Re- af- firm that you will find _____
You're not ask- ing for the world, _____

DON'T CRY OUT LOUD

Words and Music by CAROLE BAYER SAGER
and PETER ALLEN

Don't cry ___ out loud, _____ just keep it in - side, _____ learn how to
Fly high ___ and proud, _____ and if you should fall _____ re - mem - ber you

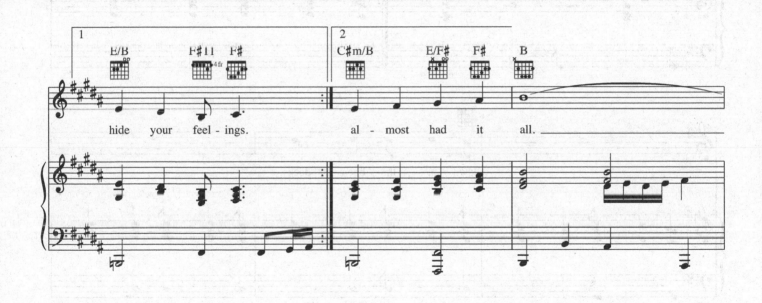

1
hide your feel - ings.

2
al - most had it all. _____

DOWN IN THE BOONDOCKS

Words and Music by
JOE SOUTH

73

DUST IN THE WIND

Words and Music by
KERRY LIVGREN

ev - 'ry - thing _ is dust in the wind.
wind.)

Repeat and Fade

Optional Ending

poco rit.

GOD ONLY KNOWS

Words and Music by BRIAN WILSON
and TONY ASHER

GOOD VIBRATIONS

Words and Music by BRIAN WILSON
and MIKE LOVE

THE GREAT PRETENDER

Words and Music by
BUCK RAM

GOODBYE TO LOVE

Words and Music by RICHARD CARPENTER
and JOHN BETTIS

GREEN ONIONS

Written by AL JACKSON, JR., LEWIS STEINBERG,
BOOKER T. JONES and STEVE CROPPER

HOW WILL I KNOW

Words and Music by GEORGE MERRILL,
SHANNON RUBICAM and NARADA MICHAEL WALDEN

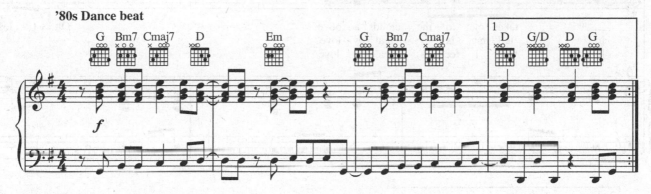

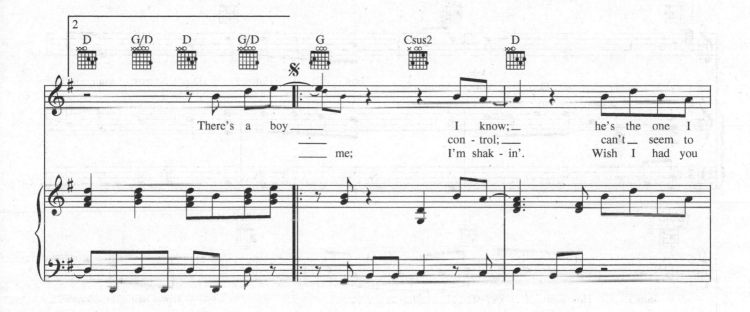

There's a boy _____ I know; _____ he's the one I
_____ con - trol; _____ I can't _____ seem to
_____ me; I'm shak - in'. Wish I had you

dream _ of.
get e - nough.
near me now.

dream _ of.   Looks in - to _____   my eyes; _____
get e - nough.   When I wake _____ from dream -
near me now.   Said there's no _____ mis - tak -

Original key: G♭ major. This edition has been transposed up one half-step to be more playable.

HERO

Words and Music by MARIAH CAREY
and WALTER AFANASIEFF

103

104

105

I AM WOMAN

Words by HELEN REDDY
Music by RAY BURTON

Moderate Rock beat

I am wom-an, hear me roar __ in num-bers too big to ig-nore, __ and I know too much to go __ back to pre-tend. __

__ 'cause I've heard it all be-fore __ and I've been down there on the floor, __ no one's

IF YOU'RE GONE

Written by ROB THOMAS

I DON'T WANT TO WAIT

Words and Music by
PAULA COLE

121

122

I HEARD IT
THROUGH THE GRAPEVINE

Words and Music by NORMAN J. WHITFIELD
and BARRETT STRONG

Moderately
N.C.

Mm. _____ I bet you're won - derin' how I knew

'bout your plans ___ to make me blue, ___ with some oth - er guy ___
but these tears ___ I can't hold in - side. ___ Los - in' you ___
son, and none ___ of what you hear. ___ But I can't help ___

ain't sup - posed to cry,
of what you see,

I HOPE YOU DANCE

Words and Music by TIA SILLERS
and MARK D. SANDERS

133

134

IF I EVER LOSE MY FAITH IN YOU

Written and Composed by
STING

140

IT'S TOO LATE

Words by TONI STERN
Music by CAROLE KING

JACK AND DIANE

Words and Music by
JOHN MELLENCAMP

Moderately

Play 3 times

A lit-tle dit-ty a-bout Jack and Di-ane,

two A-mer-i-can kids grow-in' up

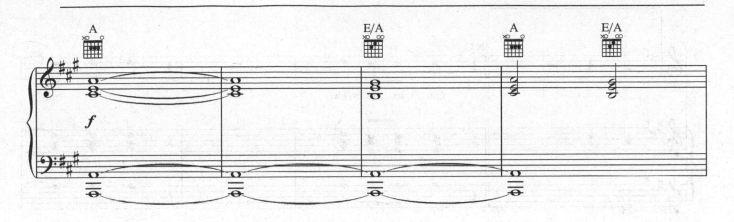

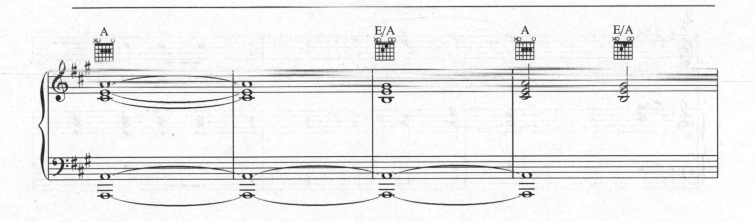

change is com - in' 'round real soon, make us wom - en and men.

C   E/A   D/A   E/A

A   E/A   D/A   A

D.S. al Coda

CODA   A   E

A lit - tle

156

JOY TO THE WORLD

Words and Music by
HOYT AXTON

LADY MARMALADE

Words and Music by BOB CREWE
and KENNY NOLAN

Moderate groove

(Hey sister, go sister, soul sister, go sister. Hey sister, go sister, soul sister, go sister.) He

met Mar-ma-lade __ down in old __ New Or-leans, __ strut-tin' her stuff __ on the street. __

163

black sat - in sheets, I swear ___ he start-ed to freak. ___

Hey, ___ hey, ___ hey ___

LET'S HEAR IT FOR THE BOY

from the Paramount Motion Picture FOOTLOOSE

Words by DEAN PITCHFORD
Music by TOM SNOW

hear it for __ the boy. __ Let's give the boy __ a hand. __

Let's

hear it for __ my bu - by, _____ you know you got __ to un - der - stand.

Oh, _____

LOOKS LIKE WE MADE IT

Words and Music by RICHARD KERR
and WILL JENNINGS

ME AND YOU AND A DOG NAMED BOO

Words and Music by
LOBO

176

MELLOW YELLOW

Words and Music by
DONOVAN LEITCH

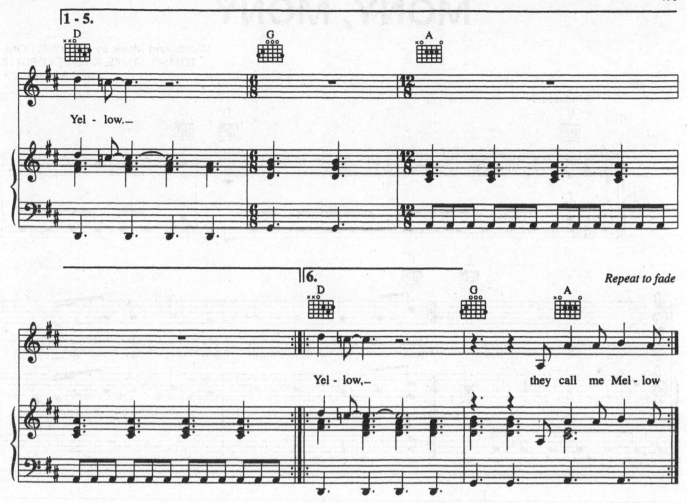

Verse 2:
I'm just mad about Fourteen,
Fourteen's mad about me.
I'm just mad about Fourteen,
She's just mad about me.

TO CHORUS:

Verse 3:
Born high, forever to fly,
Wind velocity: nil
Born high, forever to fly,
If you want your cup I will fill.

TO CHORUS:

Verse 4:
Instrumental

Verse 5:
Electrical banana
Is going to be a sudden craze.
Electrical banana
Is bound to be the very next phase.

TO CHORUS:

Verse 6:
I'm just mad about Saffron
I'm just mad about her.
I'm just mad about Saffron
She's just mad about me.

TO CHORUS:

MONY, MONY

Words and Music by BOBBY BLOOM,
TOMMY JAMES, RITCHIE CORDELL
and BO GENTRY

MOONLIGHT FEELS RIGHT

Words and Music by
MICHAEL BLACKMAN

The wind blew some luck in my di-
lay back and ob-serve the con-stel-
Instrumental
see the sun come up on Sun-day

rec - tion;   I caught it in my hands to - day.___   I
la - tions   and watch the moon___ smil - in' bright.___   I'll
morn - ing   and watch it fade the moon a - way.___   I

fi - n'lly made a trick - y French con - nec - tion; you winked and gave me your O. K.___
play the ra - di - o on south - ern sta - tions, 'cause south - ern belles are hell at night.___
guess you know I'm giv - ing you a warn - ing, 'cause me and moon are itch - ing to play.___

___ I'll take you on a trip be - side the o - cean and
___ You say you came to Bal - ti - more from Old Miss, a
___ I'll take you on a trip be - side the o - cean and

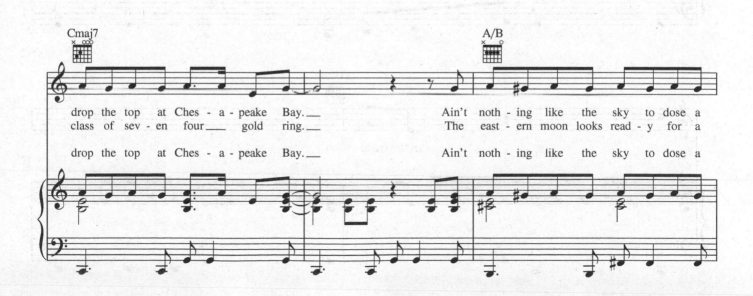

drop the top at Ches - a - peake Bay.___ Ain't noth - ing like the sky to dose a
class of sev - en four___ gold ring.___ The east - ern moon looks read - y for a

drop the top at Ches - a - peake Bay.___ Ain't noth - ing like the sky to dose a

NA NA HEY HEY KISS HIM GOODBYE

Words and Music by ARTHUR FRASHUER DALE,
PAUL ROGER LEKA and GARY CARLA

ONE SWEET DAY

Words and Music by MARIAH CAREY, WALTER AFANASIEFF,
SHAWN STOCKMAN, MICHAEL McCARY,
NATHAN MORRIS and WANYA MORRIS

RAINY DAYS AND MONDAYS

Lyrics by PAUL WILLIAMS
Music by ROGER NICHOLS

RESPECT

Words and Music by
OTIS REDDING

SHEILA

Words and Music by
TOMMY ROE

RESPECT YOURSELF

Words and Music by MACK RICE
and LUTHER INGRAM

SHOP AROUND

Words and Music by BERRY GORDY
and WILLIAM "SMOKEY" ROBINSON

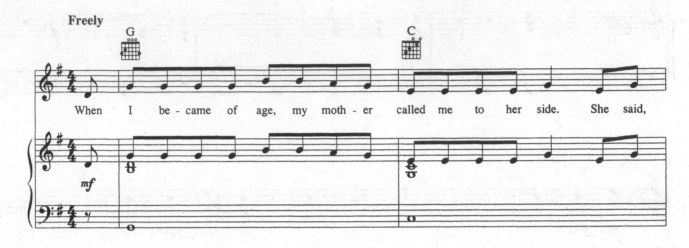

(SITTIN' ON) THE DOCK OF THE BAY

Words and Music by STEVE CROPPER
and OTIS REDDING

THE SIGN

Words and Music by buddha,
joker, jenny and linn

STAND BY ME

Words and Music by BEN E. KING,
JERRY LEIBER and MIKE STOLLER

STOP! IN THE NAME OF LOVE

Words and Music by LAMONT DOZIER,
BRIAN HOLLAND and EDWARD HOLLAND

Steadily

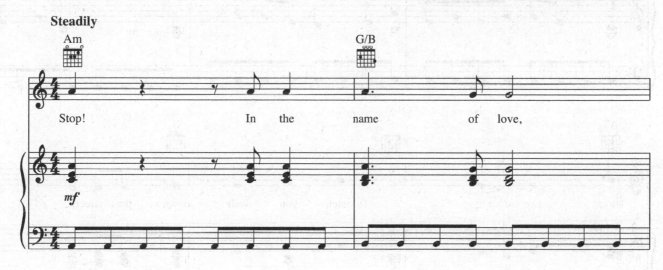

Stop!   In the   name   of   love,

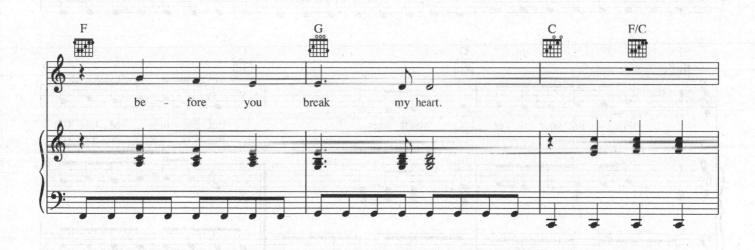

be - fore   you   break   my heart.

STOP! IN THE NAME OF LOVE

Cmaj7   Gm

Ba - by, ba - by, I'm a - ware _ of where you go   each time you

A7   F   G

leave my door. _   I watch you walk down the street, _

F   G   C

know - ing your oth - er love you'll meet. _   But this time _ be - fore you
                                                But this time _ be - fore you

G/B   F

run   to her,   leav - ing me a - lone _ and hurt, _
leave my arms   and rush off   to _   her charms, _

(Think it

SUNSHINE SUPERMAN

Words and Music by
DONOVAN LEITCH

1. Sun-shine came soft-ly through my win-dow to-day,—
(Verses 2, 3, 4 & 5 see block lyric)

could have tripped out ea-sy but I've changed my ways,—

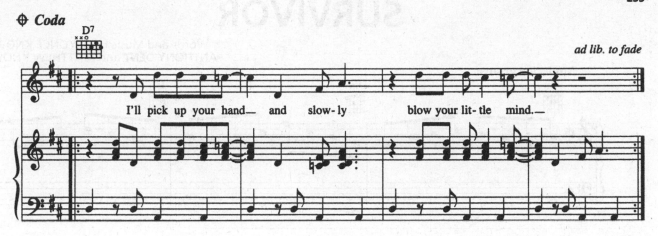

SURVIVOR

ad lib. to fade

I'll pick up your hand— and slow- ly   blow your lit- tle   mind.—

Verse 2:
Superman and Green Lantern ain't got nothing on me
I can make like a turtle and dive for pearls in the sea
You can just sit there thinking on your velvet throne
I've followed the rainbow so you can have all your own.

'Cause I've made my mind up you're going to be mine.
I'll tell you right now
Any trick in the book now baby that I can find.

Verse 3:
Everybody's hustling just to have a little scene
When I said we'd be cool I think that you know what I mean.
We stood on a beach at sunset, do you remember when?
I know a beach where baby, it never ends.

When you've made your mind up forever to be mine.
(to 3rd ending)

Verse 4:
Instrumental

Verse 5:
Superman and Green Lantern ain't got nothing on me
I can make like a turtle and dive for pearls in the sea
You can just sit there thinking on your velvet throne
I've followed the rainbow so you can have all your own.

When you've made your mind up forever to be mine.
(to 5th ending)

SURVIVOR

Words and Music by BEYONCE KNOWLES,
ANTHONY DENT and MATTHEW KNOWLES

Moderate groove

Now that you're out of my life, __ I'm so much
breathe with- out __ you, I'm in-

bet- ter. You thought that I'd be weak with- out __ you but I'm strong-er. You thought that I'd be
hal- in'. You thought I could-n't see with- out __ you, per- fect vi- sion. You thought I could-n't

broke __ with- out __ you but I'm rich- er. You thought that I'd be sad with- out __ you, I laugh
last __ with- out __ you but I'm last- in'. You thought that I would die with- out __ you but I'm

Original key: Ab minor. This edition has been transposed up one half-step to be more playable.

TEARIN' UP MY HEART

Words and Music by MAX MARTIN
and KRISTIAN LUNDIN

It's tear-in' up my heart when I'm ___ with you, ___ but when we are a-
part I feel ___ it, too. ___ And no mat-ter what ___ I ___ do ___
I feel ___ the pain ___ with or with-out ___ you. ___

SWEET DREAMS
(Are Made of This)

Words and Music by DAVID A. STEWART
and ANNIE LENNOX

249

THE SWEETEST DAYS

Words and Music by JON LIND,
WENDY WALDMAN and PHIL GALDSTON

TEQUILA

By CHUCK RIO

TOP OF THE WORLD

Words and Music by JOHN BETTIS
and RICHARD CARPENTER

Such a feel - in's com - in' o - ver me. _____
Some - thing in _____ the wind has learned _____ my name. _____

THANK YOU

Words and Music by PAUL HERMAN
and DIDO ARMSTRONG

Vocal written one octave higher than sung.

Original key: G# minor. This edition has been transposed up one half-step to be more playable.

Push the door; I'm home _ at _ last, _ and I'm soak - ing through _ and through..

TOUCH ME IN THE MORNING

Words and Music by RONALD MILLER
and MICHAEL MASSER

TRACES

Words and Music by J.R. COBB
and BUDDY BUIE

THE TRACKS OF MY TEARS

Words and Music by WILLIAM "SMOKEY" ROBINSON,
WARREN MOORE and MARVIN TARPLIN

VISION OF LOVE

Words and Music by MARIAH CAREY
and BEN MARGULIES

WALK LIKE AN EGYPTIAN

Words and Music by
LIAM STERNBERG

1. All the old paint - ings on ___ the
2. All the ba - zaar men by ___ the
3.–7. *(See additional lyrics)*

tomb, they do ___ the sand dance, don't you know. If they move too
Nile, they got ___ the mon - ey on ___ a bet. Gold croc - o -

quick, (oh ___ way oh,) they're fall - ing down like a dom - i - no.
diles, (oh ___ way oh,) they snap ___ their teeth

Additional Lyrics

3. The blond waitresses take their trays.
They spin around and they cross the floor.
They've got the moves, oh way oh.
You drop your drink, then they bring you more.

4. All the schoolkids so sick of books,
They like the punk and the metal band.
Then the buzzer rings, oh way oh,
They're walking like an Egyptian.

5. Slide your feet up the street, bend your back.
Shift your arm, then you pull it back.
Life's hard, you know, oh way oh,
So strike a pose on a Cadillac.

6. If you want to find all the cops,
They're hanging out in the donut shop.
They sing and dance, oh way oh.
They spin the club, cruise down the block.

7. All the Japanese with their yen,
The party boys call the Kremlin.
And the Chinese know, oh way oh,
They walk the line like Egyptians.

WALK RIGHT IN

Words and Music by GUS CANNON
and H. WOODS

WALKING ON BROKEN GLASS

Words and Music by
ANNIE LENNOX

WE GOT THE BEAT

Words and Music by
CHARLOTTE CAFFEY

See the peo - ple walk - ing down the street;
See the kids just get - ting out of school.
Go - go mu - sic real - ly makes us dance.

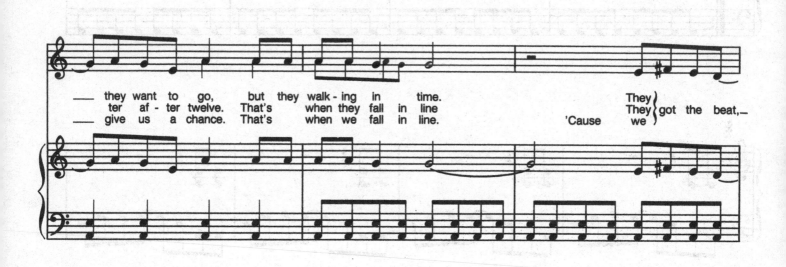

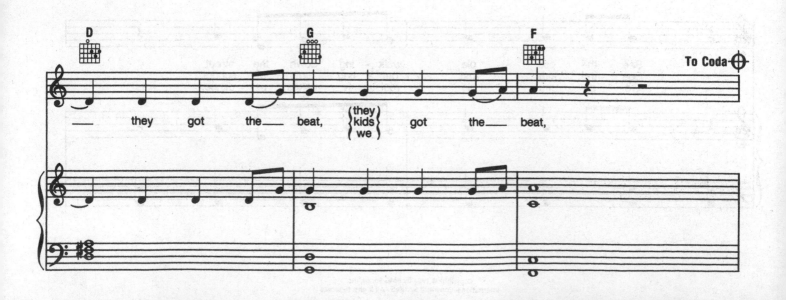

yeah,   they got the beat.   yeah,   kids got the beat.

WATER RUNS DRY

Words and Music by
BABYFACE

WHAT'S GOING ON

Words and Music by MARVIN GAYE,
AL CLEVELAND and RENALDO BENSON

313

A WHITER SHADE OF PALE

Words and Music by KEITH REID
and GARY BROOKER

WHY DO FOOLS FALL IN LOVE

Words and Music by MORRIS LEVY
and FRANKIE LYMON

WINCHESTER CATHEDRAL

Words and Music by
GEOFF STEPHENS

YOU SANG TO ME

Words and Music by CORY ROONEY
and MARC ANTHONY

All the while __ you were __ in front __ of me __ I nev-er

YESTERDAY ONCE MORE

Words and Music by JOHN BETTIS
and RICHARD CARPENTER

Moderate Ballad

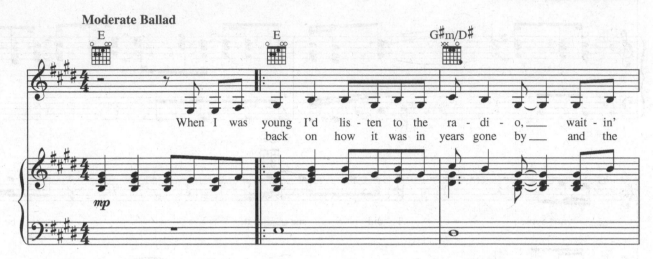

When I was young I'd lis-ten to the ra-di-o,___ wait-in'
back on how it was in years gone by ___ and the

for my fa-v'rite songs.___ When they played, I'd sing a - long;___
good times that I had, ___ makes to-day seem rath-er sad;___

___ it made me smile.___ Those were such
___ so much has changed.___ It was

YOU KEEP ME HANGIN' ON

Words and Music by EDWARD HOLLAND,
LAMONT DOZIER and BRIAN HOLLAND

Set me free. Why don't _ you, ba - by? { Get out my life. } Why don't _
{ Let me be. }
_ you, ba - by? 'Cause you don't _ real - ly love _ me, you just keep _

This edition has been transposed up one half-step from the original recording to be more playable.

YOU'RE THE INSPIRATION

Words and Music by PETER CETERA
and DAVID FOSTER

1. You know our love was meant to be
2. (See additional lyrics)

the kind of love ___ that lasts ___ for-

ev - er. ___ And I want you here with

Additional Lyrics

2. And I know (yes, I know)
That it's plain to see
We're so in love when we're together.
Now I know (now I know)
That I need you here with me
From tonight until the end of time.
You should know everywhere I go;
Always on my mind, you're in my heart, in my soul.
(To Chorus:)